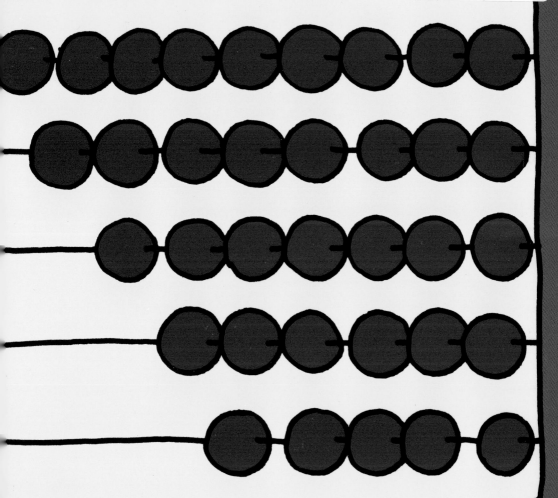

this book belongs to:

for Barnaby

This edition published 2008 by Walker Books Ltd
87 Vauxhall Walk, London SE11 5HJ
10 9 8 7 6 5 4 3 2 1
© 1973, 2008 Jan Pieńkowski

Printed in China
British Library Cataloguing in Publication Data is available
ISBN 978-1-4063-1436-6
www.walkerbooks.co.uk

WALKER BOOKS
AND SUBSIDIARIES
LONDON · BOSTON · SYDNEY · AUCKLAND

NUMBERS

Jan Pieńkowski

1

one leopard

2
two cows

3

three witches

4
four ducks

5

five sheep

6
six robins

7

seven soldiers

8
eight toadstools

9

nine tulips

10
ten apples

how many?

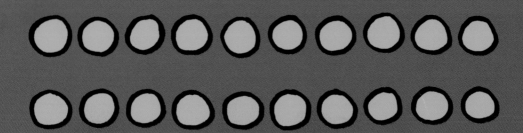

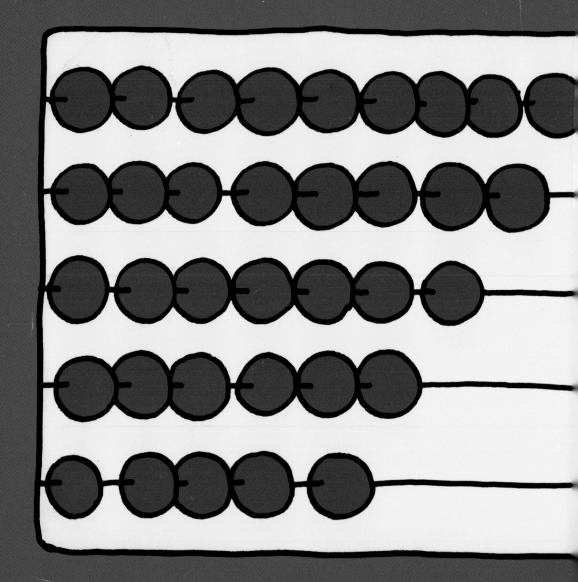